Sword Fighting

A Scripture Memory Curriculum for Home and School

By
Karyn Henley

Allen Thomas
PUBLISHING

ALLEN THOMAS PUBLISHING COMPANY
Post Office Box 40269
Nashville, Tennessee   37204

10 9 8 7 6 5 4 3 2 1

For more information on how to order additional copies of *Sword Fighting*, or information about Karyn Henley's teacher training workshops, write to the Allen Thomas Publishing Company.

ISBN 1-879541-21-1

TABLE OF CONTENTS

SCRIPTURE CHART

Lesson 1: "I have hidden your word in my heart that I might not sin against you." Psalm 119:11

Lesson 2: "Be self-controlled." I Peter 1:13

Lesson 3: "My help comes from the Lord, the Maker of heaven and earth." Psalm 121:2

Lesson 4: "Be quick to listen and slow to speak." James 1:19

Lesson 5: "Hope does not disappoint us, because God has poured out his love into our hearts by the Holy Spirit whom he has given us." Romans 5:5

Lesson 6: "By the grace of God, I am what I am." I Corinthians 15:10

Lesson 7: Always give thanks to God the Father for everything." Ephesians 5:20

Lesson 8: "Whatever you do, work at it with all your heart, as working for the Lord." Colossians 3:23

Lesson 9: "Do everything without complaining or arguing." Philippians 2:14

Lesson 10: "Pray always." I Thessolonians 5:17

Lesson 11: "All things work together for good to them who love God." Romans 8:28

Lesson 12: "Give thanks to the Lord, for he is good." Psalm 136:1.

Lesson 13: "There is a time for everything." Ecclesiastes 3:1

Lesson 14: "Rejoice with those who rejoice; mourn with those who mourn." Romans 12:15

Lesson 15: "Children obey your parents in the Lord, for this is right." Ephesians 6:1

Lesson 16: "Each man should give what he has decided in his heart to give, not reluctantly or under compulsion, for God loves a cheerful giver." II Corinthians 9:7

INTRODUCTION

Options for Using *Sword Fighting*

Option 1: School Year Schedule

This option will cover the entire curriculum in 36 weeks, corresponding with a typical school year.

Home School or Private School
- One theme each week.
- One reading for each of the five school days.
- Activities as desired.
- "Sword fight" memory practice during the week

Sunday School
- One reading during class on Sunday, with activities as desired.
- Four readings done with family during the week at home, plus optional activities as desired.
- "Sword fight" practice in class and at home during the week.

Option 2: Full 52-week (one year) Schedule

This option will cover the entire 36-lesson curriculum in three years.

Home School
- One theme each month for 12 months.
- One reading for each week of the month.
- Activities during the month as desired.
- "Sword fight" practice weekly.

Sunday School
- One theme a month for 12 months.
- One reading each class time, with activities as desired.

- "Sword fight" practice weekly.
- Additional activities for class time may be needed. These can be found in supplemental activity books. For younger grades, the *First Hand* series is suggested.

WHAT IS SWORD FIGHTING?

Its Basis

Sword Fighting is designed to be a training ground for one aspect of spiritual warfare: temptation. It is based on three scriptures:

- "Take . . . the sword of the Spirit which is the word of God." Ephesians 6:17
- The temptations of Jesus, Matthew 4:1-11, in which Jesus responded to temptation by quoting the Scriptures, "It is written . . ."
- David's statement: "I have hidden thy word in my heart that I might not sin against thee." Psalm 119:11

Sword Fighting is designed to intertwine the child's group learning with teaching done at home during the week. Parents can be a major part of this training, even learning the verses themselves as a family project. However, even if the child's parents are not involved, he will still gain benefits from his group experience, and can learn the scriptures on his own.

Its Focus

Sword Fighting is a game of scripture memory that can be played once a few scriptures are learned. Each week, a sword is cut out of paper or half of a sheet of posterboard. The scripture is written on it, and it is posted in a visible place at home. The child practices the scripture until it is memorized.

After a few verses are memorized, their corresponding themes are written on slips of paper. The slips are folded and placed in a bag or hat. One person draws a theme and reads it. For example, "Honesty." The other person "draws his sword" (figuratively) and quotes the verse, "Do not lie to each other." (Colossians 3:9) Then the two people switch roles: the second person draws and the first person "fights."

The point is: when you are tempted to lie, how do you "fight" that temptation? Like Jesus did: "It is written" "do not lie to each other." Or when you are tempted to be disrespectful, how do you "fight?" Quote the verse found with the theme "respect." Etc.

Its Format

Theme: There are currently 36 weeks of themes and verses corresponding to 36 weeks of the school year. (See Options to see how to use the themes for an entire year.) Most themes in *Sword Fighting* are character qualities that show up in actions. Christmas, Thanksgiving and Easter weeks are based on Biblical events and scriptures that support those themes.

Verse: With each theme, there is a memory verse, a "sword," to practice "fighting" with.

Readings: To support the theme and verse are five suggested Bible readings. One reading is to be used to introduce the theme and illustrate how real people revealed or did not reveal the character quality. The four other short readings are to be done during the week.

Questions: A list of questions accompanies each theme. Questions are very important to start discussion. And it is important to listen and set a warm, accepting atmosphere in order to encourage the children to feel free to confide their true feelings and experiences and to see how God really can work in their daily lives.

Activities: There is also, with each theme, a list of optional activities that the parent and the person leading the children can choose from to support the theme. The most important parts of this curriculum are the memory verses, Bible readings and discussion. The activities are available as a vehicle to facilitate conversation (which is often easier and more natural when the hands are busy), and to inject some fun and action into the training, while reinforcing the theme in some way.

LESSON 1

Theme: Temptation

Verse: "I have hidden your word in my heart that I might not sin against you." Psalm 119:11 (Write this verse on paper swords, one for each child.)

Reading 1: Matthew 4:1-4—Jesus is Tempted in the Desert

Questions:

- Did the devil tell Jesus the truth? There are two spiritual kingdoms. What are they? (Light and darkness.)
- What do you know about them?
- Is the war between them real?
- Why do things go wrong in the world?
- What is our spiritual armor? (Read Ephesians 6:10ff)
- What is salvation?
- What is our shield?
- What is our sword?
- How did Jesus use the word of God?
- How can we use the word of God like a sword?
- Is temptation sin?
- Tell of a time you were tempted or someone you know was tempted.
- Is it easy to resist temptation?
- What kinds of things tempt people?
- What kinds of things tempt you?

Reading 2: Matthew 4:5-7—Jesus is Tempted in the Desert

Reading 3: Matthew 4:8-11—Jesus is Tempted in the Desert

Reading 4: Genesis 4:7—God Warns Cain

Reading 5: I Corinthians 10:13—God Provides a Way Out

Activities

Sword Fight

Talk about how the Sword of the Spirit is the Word of God. What scripture from the Word was written on the sword today? Write "Why are we learning the Word?" on a slip of paper. This is the first playing piece for the Sword Fight game in coming weeks. Practice with one person asking the question on the slip, and another answering by quoting the scripture on the sword for today. Then switch roles, the second person asking the question, and the first quoting the scripture.

Shields

Each child makes a shield out of poster board or cardboard and decorates it with markers and/or stickers. Talk about "symbols"—pictures that have a meaning.

Examples:
- cross = Jesus
- sun = light
- lion = courage
- crown = authority
- dove = Holy Spirit
- olive leaf = peace.

What symbol would you choose to represent yourself?

Manna

Read Deuteronomy. 8:1-5. Make manna. Set oven to 350°. Let children help mix ¼ c. melted margarine, ¼ c. honey, ½ tsp. cinnamon, and 1 tsp. vanilla in one bowl. They put 2 c. buttermilk baking mix in the other bowl. Add the margarine mixture, and then add ¼ c. milk. Stir. Each child rolls a ball of the dough and places it on the cookie sheet. He presses it down a little bit. Bake for 10 min. Eat.

Water Play

Discover the properties of water by melting ice and then heating it to steam. Make "rain" by holding a metal bowl of ice over a steaming tea kettle or boiling pan of water. Read Deuteronomy 6:16. Read about Massah, Exodus 17:3-7.

Cause and Effect

Line up dominoes and tap the first one to see all of them tumble. Sin affects our lives. What are some of the effects of sin?

Idols

Cut out pictures from magazines or catalogues of things that we could focus our lives on—things that could become idols to us.

Ads

Look in magazines and catalogues to find lies that we are tempted to believe about products.

LESSON 2

Theme: Self Control

"Be self-controlled." I Peter 1:13
(Write this verse on paper swords, one for each
child. Older children can write it on the sword
themselves.)

Reading 1:   I Samuel 24—David Spares Saul's Life

Questions:

- What is self control?
- Tell about a time when you or someone you
  know showed self control.
- What is so hard about self control?
- What else can control a person?
- Read Proverbs 25:28. Why is this true?

Reading 2:   Genesis 42—Joseph's Secret

Reading 3:   I Kings 21—King Ahab Pouts

Reading 4:   Daniel 1—Daniel and the King's Food

Reading 5:   John 18:1-11 and Luke 22:47-51—Peter Cuts
off the Servant's Ear

Activities

Sword Fight

Write the theme for this lesson on a slip of paper. Place that slip of paper, along with the slip of paper from the last lessons' sword fight, in a bag or hat. One person draws a theme and reads it aloud. The other person "draws his sword" (figuratively) and quotes the verse that goes with that theme. Then they switch roles: the second person draws and the first person quotes the corresponding scripture. See the Introduction under Its Focus for a complete explanation.

Secret Code

Let children make up a secret code by deciding on a shape or symbol to represent each letter of the alphabet. They can write their names in this code, write the memory verse in this code, write other messages in this code. Talk about how keeping secrets requires self discipline. What secret was Joseph keeping? Ask if they can tell about a time when it was hard to keep a secret.

Flavors

Cut small bites of different kinds of foods with different distinctive flavors, such as pickles (dill or sweet), apples, cheese, grapes, peanuts, etc. Have children close their eyes while you put one bite into each of their mouths. Let them guess what it is. Discuss self discipline in regard to food and eating.

Dams

In a sand box or dirt area of your yard, let the children dig a river bed. Line it with plastic from a trash bag, weighted down with rocks. Fill the "river" with water. Now the children build a dam across the river, using sticks or mud or toy blocks, or whatever their creativity can devise. Discuss the use of the dam to control the water. Discuss how we control ourselves. What does it feel like to lose control?

Ears

Pretend you are zoologists. You are researching types of ears that different animals have, and why they might have that certain type of ear. Each child can take paper and crayons, markers, or pencils and look at animal pictures in books, nature magazines, or encyclopedias and draw several types of animal ears, writing under each one the name of the animal. Discuss why God may have given the animal an ear like that. Discuss self control in regard to things we might have opportunity to listen to.

Secrets

Play the game "Gossip," if you have several children. Whisper some phrase quickly into one child's ear. He whispers it into the next child's ear. The last child to receive the whisper tells out loud what he heard. Was it the same as the first whisper? Discuss the self control needed to keep a secret.

LESSON 3

Theme: Confidence/Self-Pity

Verse: "My help comes from the Lord, the Maker of heaven and earth." Psalm 121:2
(Write this verse on paper swords, one for each child. Older children can write on swords themselves.)

Reading 1: Genesis 23—Moses says "I Can't"

Questions:

- What is confidence?
- Why do you think Moses said, "I can't?"
- Tell of a time when you or someone else needed confidence.
- Why might someone not have confidence?
- What is self pity?
- Did you ever feel sorry for yourself?
- What would you suggest to a friend who was feeling sorry for himself?

Reading 2: I Kings 19:1-18—Elijah Hides

Reading 3: Jeremiah 1:4-10—God Chooses Jeremiah

Reading 4: Luke 15:11-32—Brother of the Prodigal Son (self pity)

Reading 5: Jonah 4—Jonah and the Vine (self pity)

Activities

Sword Fight

Write the theme for this lesson on a slip of paper. Place that slip of paper, along with the slips of paper from the previous lessons' sword fights, in a bag or hat. One person draws a theme and reads it aloud. The other person "draws his sword" (figuratively) and quotes the verse that goes with that theme. Then they switch roles: the second person draws and the first person quotes the corresponding scripture. See the introduction under "Its Focus" for a complete explanation.

Tug of War

Get a rope. Divide into teams. Wear gloves. Mark a line in the grass or dirt. The center of the rope goes over the line. Each team holds to a different end of the rope, and at the signal to start, they each pull. The team that can pull the other over the line first wins. Discuss what happens if the team tells itself, "I can," and what happens if the team tells itself, "I can't." Can we always do what we think we can do? Can we always do what God wants us to do? Why? Whose strength never fails?

Arm Wrestle

Two people place elbows on a table. Each person uses the same arm. They clasp hands. Each tries to push the other's arm over by pushing with that one hand, not using the other hand, and not lifting the elbow off the table. Discussion is the same as above. Whose strength never fails?

Thumb Wrestle

Similar to the arm wrestle, except that fists are on the table, holding hands with thumbs up. Try to push the opponent's thumb down. Discussion is the same as above. Whose strength never fails?

Cave Model

Using clay or play dough, make a model of a cave. Discuss the reading of Elijah.

Macaroni Name

The children write their names on construction paper, then draw over the letters with glue. They put macaroni on the glue lines. Discuss what God's purpose was for Moses and Elijah and Jeremiah. Does God have a special purpose for our lives? What might his purpose for you be?

String Vine

Cut leaf shapes out of construction paper. Cut a long piece of string. This is the vine. Put leaves on the vine by sandwiching the string between two leaves and stapling them. Place leaves all along the vine. You can write one word of the memory verse on each leaf section if you want. Discuss the story of Jonah and the vine.

Sun and Shade

Choose an outdoor spot that has shade and sun. Set up a thermometer in the sun, and one in the shade. Is there a difference in temperature? Stand in the sun and then in the shade. Do you feel a difference? Discuss Jonah and the vine.

LESSON 4

Theme: Listening

Verse: "Be quick to listen and slow to speak." James
1:19
(Write this verse on paper swords, one for each
child. Older children can write it on swords
themselves.)

Reading 1:   John 10:11 ff—Hearing God's Voice

Questions:

  • How can someone hear God's voice?

  • What are some other voices we hear, and what
    do they tell us?

  • Who is it important to listen to?

  • Why is it important to listen?

  • What does the verse mean when it says, "slow
    to speak?"

Reading 2:   Luke 10:38-42—Mary and Martha

Reading 3:   I Samuel 3—God Talks to Samuel

Reading 4:   Matthew 7:24-27—Wise and Foolish Men

Reading 5:   Acts 23:12-24—Paul's Nephew Hears a Plot

Activities

Sword Fight

Write the theme for this lesson on a slip of paper. Place that slip of paper, along with the slips of paper from the previous lessons' sword fights, in a bag or hat. One person draws a theme and reads it aloud. The other person "draws his sword" (figuratively) and quotes the verse that goes with that theme. Then they switch roles: the second person draws and the first person quotes the corresponding scripture. See the introduction under "Its Focus" for a complete explanation.

Whose Voice

One child stands in the center of the room. The others make a wide circle around him. One child speaks, disguising his voice if he wants, and the child in the center tries to tell who it is. Discuss the voice Samuel heard. What would you have done? How did he know it was God? How do we hear God?

Erosion

Build a landscape of sand or dirt. Build a landscape of rocks. Pour water over each one with a gardener's sprinkling can or a spray bottle or with water spraying from a garden hose. What happens to each one? Discuss erosion. Discuss the wise man and the fool. Discuss hearing and obeying.

Sounds

Let children record a cassette of ordinary sounds such as barking dog, piano, sound of feet going up stairs, door squeaking open, water dripping, phone ringing, typewriter or computer keyboard, etc. Play these for someone who has not heard them and let them guess what the sounds are. This is fun for older children to do for younger children. If the children are young, you could make the tape for them and let them guess. Discuss listening.

Funny Ears

Draw faces on paper, but do not draw the ears. Now cut ears out of magazine pictures and glue them on the pictures you have drawn. Discuss listening.

Paper Ears

Draw big ears (these can be human ears or animal ears) on construction paper or posterboard. Make a headbands by cutting strips of paper or posterboard about one inch wide. If a strip is not long enough to fit around the head, staple two strips together to make it long enough. Now staple the ears to each side of the headband. They can either hang down or stick up, as you choose. Discuss listening.

LESSON 5

Theme: Hope

Verse: "Hope does not disappoint us, because God has poured out his love into our hearts by the Holy Spirit whom he has given us." Romans 5:5 (Write this verse on paper swords, one for each child. Older children can write the verses themselves.)

Reading 1:   I Samuel 1:1-20—Hannah Hopes for a Baby

Questions:

- What is hope?
- What do you hope for?
- What kind of hope does the verse talk about?
- Is hope different from wishing?
- Have you ever been disappointed? Tell about it.

Reading 2:   Luke 2:22-33—Simeon Hoped to see Baby Jesus

Reading 3:   Genesis 40—Joseph Hopes for Release

Reading 4:   Acts 1:1-14—Apostles Wait for the Gift

Reading 5:   Luke 8:42b-48—A Woman Touches Jesus' Hem

Activities

Sword Fight

Write the theme for this lesson on a slip of paper. Place that slip of paper, along with the slips of paper from the previous lessons' sword fights, in a bag or hat. One person draws a theme and reads it aloud. The other person "draws his sword" (figuratively) and quotes the verse that goes with that theme. Then they switch roles: the second person draws and the first person quotes the corresponding scripture. See the introduction under "Its Focus" for a complete explanation.

Paper Plate Puppet

Choose one of the readings to do a puppet skit for. Make puppets by drawing each character's face on the bottom of a paper plate. Staple each paper plate to another paper plate, insides together, leaving it open at the bottom of the "face," so the child's hand can fit inside. You can glue on hair, and decorate it in other ways if you like. Practice the story and perform it for someone. Discuss hope.

Praying Hand Prints

Use play dough (which you can make by mixing 2 cups of flour with 1 cup of salt and enough water to make it easy to knead). Flatten a circle of play dough and make a hand print by pressing a hand, fingers together as if praying, into the dough. Let it dry. Paint it if you want. Talk about Hannah's prayer and hope, and about the children's hopes and prayers.

Joseph in Prison

Draw a line down the center of an index card. Leave a 1" margin on each end of the card. Draw a face or figure to represent Joseph on one side of the center line. Draw bars on the other side. Now hold another index card perpendicular to the center line. Looking at this card, move your face closer to it until your nose touches the card. Watch Joseph move into prison. Discuss Joseph's situation, and situations we might be in where there might not look like there's hope for escape.

Fold and Cut Doves

Fold a piece of white typing paper or construction paper in half horizontally. Draw the figure of a dove, with its belly along the fold. Cut out along the drawn lines, but do not cut along the fold. Tape or staple the upper body together, folding wings out. Hang on string or tape to a straw to use as a puppet. Discuss the Holy Spirit who came as a dove when Jesus was baptized, and for whom the apostles waited. Discuss Reading 4.

Mystery Bag

Place small, familiar household items into a pillow case or sack. Use things a child would know, the younger the child, the simpler the item, such as a comb, an apple, etc. For an older child, make it more challenging, such as a battery, a coin, an acorn, etc. Discuss touching, and the woman who touched Jesus' hem. Discuss hopes.

LESSON 6

Theme: Humility

Verse: "By the grace of God, I am what I am."
I Corinthians 15:10
(Write this verse on paper swords, one for each child. Older children can write it themselves.)

Reading 1: Genesis 11:1-9—Tower of Babel

Questions:

- What is it to be boastful or proud?
- What is it to be humble?
  (One definition: realizing there is someone greater than yourself.)
- Who is the greatest? Why?
- Why do you think people want to boast?

Reading 2: John 3:22-26, 30-31—John the Baptist

Reading 3: Acts 12:19-25—King Herod

Reading 4: Acts 14:8-18—A Crowd Bows to Paul

Reading 5: II Kings 5:1-14—Naaman

Activities

Sword Fight

Write the theme for this lesson on a slip of paper. Place that slip of paper, along with the slips of paper from the previous lessons' sword fights, in a bag or hat. One person draws a theme and reads it aloud. The other person "draws his sword" (figuratively) and quotes the verse that goes with that theme. Then they switch roles: the second person draws and the first person quotes the corresponding scripture. See the introduction under "Its Focus" for a complete explanation.

Box Tower

Using boxes, large or small, build a tower. If there is a large group of you, try to build an archway, using one stone in the center of the top to be the keystone on which the pressure of the sides of the arch rests. Talk about the Tower of Babel. Talk about humility.

Block Tower

Build a tower out of blocks. Discuss the Tower of Babel and humility.

Toothpick Tower

Using toothpicks and glue, build a tower. Discuss the Tower of Babel and humility.

Popsicle Stick Tower

Using glue and popsicle sticks or craft sticks, build a tower. Discuss the Tower of Babel and humility.

Insect Collection

Go outdoors and collect insects. Talk about what John the Baptist ate: locusts and wild honey. Discuss Reading 2 and humility.

Reflecting Light

Using a mirror or shiny metal (like a shiny spoon) and a light source, bounce reflections of light off the mirror or metal and onto ceiliings and walls. If there is a group, give each person a mirror or shiny metal object. Everyone reflects spots of light. Try to guess which person is making which reflection. Read Proverbs 27:21 and 27:2. Discuss Reading 3 and humility.

Dip Picture

Fill a sink, tub, bucket or wide pan with water. Using water color paints, paint a design on typing paper. Then dip the paper into the water to make a running paint design. Set it outside or on newspaper to dry. Discuss Naaman and humility.

LESSON 7

Theme: Gratitude

Verse: "Always give thanks to God the Father for
              everything." Ephesians 5:20
              (Write this verse on paper swords, one for each
              child. Older children can write it themselves.)

Reading 1: Luke 17:11-19—Ten Lepers

Questions:

- What is gratitude?
- Why is gratitude important?
- How can a person show gratitude?
- Tell something you are grateful for.

Reading 2: I Chronicles 16:1-3, 7-36
              David's Song at the Return of the Ark

Reading 3: Acts 27:27-44—Paul on the Shipwreck

Reading 4: Luke 2:36-38—Anna's Thanks for Baby Jesus

Reading 5: Mark 6:30-44—Jesus Gives Thanks

Activities

Sword Fight

Write the theme for this lesson on a slip of paper, along with the slips of paper from the previous lessons' sword fights, in a bag or hat. One person draws a theme and reads it aloud. The other person "draws his sword" (figuratively) and quotes the verse that goes with that theme. Then they switch roles: the second person draws and the first person quotes the corresponding scripture. See the introduction under "Its Focus" for a complete explanation.

Song of Thanks

Have children write their own song of thanks like David did. Discuss gratitude.

Ship Design

Challenge the children to find materials that would make a small model ship that floats. They can try cardboard boxes, foil, clay or play dough, or wood, or Ivory soap, or styrofoam, etc. Try making a paper sail. Discuss Paul's shipwreck and gratitude.

Thumb and Fingerprints

Using ink or damp watercolor paint, make fingerprints on paper. Compare each person's fingerprints. Use a magnifying glass. Discuss gratitude for the way God has made us each as individuals.

Thank You Cards

Think of someone you can thank for something they've done. (Even just a thank you for being my friend, or dad, or grandmother.) Fold a piece of paper and make a thank you card and send it to that person. Discuss gratitude.

Loaves and Fishes Dinner

Make and share a loaves and fishes dinner. Use fish sticks and refrigerated roll dough if you need to, or if you can go fishing and catch the fish yourselves, that's even better. Make it as plain or as simple as you want. Discuss Reading 5.

LESSON 8

Theme: Dependability

Verse: "Whatever you do, work at it with all your heart, as working for the Lord." Colossians 3:23
(Write this verse on paper swords, one for each child. Older children can write it themselves.)

Reading 1: Genesis 37:1-27—Joseph Goes to Find his Brothers

Questions:
- What does "dependable" mean?
- What is a dependable person like?
- Tell about someone you know who is dependable.
- Tell how you are dependable.
- Why is it important to be dependable?
- Is it always easy to be dependable?

Reading 2: Matthew 21:28-32—Two Sons and a Vineyard

Reading 3: John 10:11-13—A Hired Man and the Shepherd

Reading 4: Genesis 39:20-40:23—Butler is not Dependable

Reading 5: Matthew 21:1-7—Disciples get a Donkey for Jesus

Activities

Sword Fight

Write the theme for this lesson on a slip of paper. Place that slip of paper, along with the slips of paper from the previous lessons' sword fights, in a bag or hat. One person draws a theme and reads it aloud. The other person "draws his sword" (figuratively) and quotes the verse that goes with that theme. Then they switch roles: the second person draws and the first person quotes the corresponding scripture. See the introduction under "Its Focus" for a complete explanation.

Mazes

Have each person draw a maze. Then trade mazes and try to work the maze you have been given. Discuss David's travels as he hunted for his brothers. Discuss dependability.

Window Garden

Plant seeds in paper cups or other small containers and place them in a window where you can care for them and watch them grow. Discuss the two sons and the vineyard. Discuss dependability.

Weeding

Go outdoors to weed and water a garden. This may be done for a neighbor or someone who needs help in their garden. Discuss the two sons and the vineyard. Discuss dependability.

Act it Out

Act out one of the readings. Discuss dependability.

Fruit Salad

Buy and prepare different fruits to make a fruit
salad. Each person gets to help peel, or slice, or
add, or mix. Eat it afterwards. Discuss dependability in our tasks.

LESSON 9

Theme: Contentment

Verse: "Do everything without complaining or argu-
               ing." Philippians 2:14
               (Write this verse on paper swords, one for each
               child. Older children can write it themselves.)

Reading 1:   I Samuel 16—David Content to be the Harpist

Questions:
- If a person is content, what is he like?
- If you have a pet, what is it like when it is
  content?
- What is your pet like when it is discontent?
- What is a baby like when he is content?
- What is a baby like when he is discontent?
- Why is it important to be content?
- Does that mean you can never say it when you
  are angry or sad or when there's a problem of
  some kind?
- What is the opposite of being content?
- What makes your life rich—meaning good,
  happy, full, satisfying?

Reading 2:   Numbers 11—Israelites Grumble

Reading 3:   Genesis 13— Abraham's and Lot's Men Argue

Reading 4:   Luke 12:16-21—Bigger Barns

Reading 5:   Philippians 4:10-13—Paul's Contentment

Activities

Sword Fight

Write the theme for this lesson on a slip of paper. Place that slip of apper, along with the slips of paper from the previous lessons' sword fights, in a bag or hat. One person draws a theme and reads it aloud. The other person "draws his sword" (figuratively) and quotes the verse that goes with that theme. Then they switch roles: the second person draws and the first person quotes the corresponding scripture. See the introduction under "Its Focus" for a complete explanation.

Praise Songs

Children write their own praise song(s). Discuss contentment.

Harps

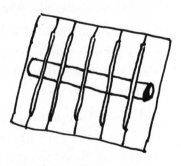

Cut four inch squares out of heavy cardboard. Make slits along each of two sides. Stretch rubber bands around the cardboard, running them through the slits. Slip a drinking straw under the rubber bands on one side. Play as a harp. Discuss David's contentment at being the harpist when he had already been anointed as king.

Glass Band

> The children fill glasses to different levels with water. Then they gently tap on the glasses with a plastic spoon, and arrange them from low to high. Challenge them to play a simple song. They can add water or pour some out as they need to in order to get the right notes. Discuss Reading 1.

Barn Raising

> Get as large a box as you can. Open the flaps on one end and tape them into a roof shape. Color or paint the box to look like a barn. Cut a door in it. Discuss Reading 4 and contentment.

Paper Bag Sheep

> Stuff a small paper bag with newspaper. Staple the end closed. Staple or tape a rectangle of white construction paper or manila paper onto this end to be the head. Color eyes and nose on it. Glue cotton balls all over the paper bag. Clip clothespins to the bottom where the legs should be. Discuss David, the shepherd boy, and harp player. Discuss contentment.

Collection

> Start or continue a collection of the child's choice. Suggestions: rock collection, leaf collection, pressed flower collection, insect collection, shell collection, etc. Discuss the farmer's bigger barns, and contentment.

LESSON 10

Theme: Prayerfulness

Verse: "Pray always." I Thessalonians 5:17
(Write this verse on paper swords, one for each child. Older children can write it themselves.)

Reading 1:   Daniel 6—Daniel Prays

Questions:

- Why do we pray?
- Where can we pray?
- When can we pray?
- How can we pray?
- Does God always answer our prayers? He can answer "yes," "no," or "wait."
- Why might God answer "no?"
- Why might God answer "wait?"
- Tell about a time when God answered your prayer.

Reading 2:   Luke 18:9-14—Pharisee's and Tax Collector's Prayers

Reading 3:   Matthew 6:5-13—The Lord's Prayer

Reading 4:   I Kings 18:16-39—Elijah on Mt. Carmel

Reading 5:   Luke 18:1-8—The Persistent Widow

Activities

Sword Fight

Write the theme for this lesson on a slip of paper. Place that slip of paper, along with the slips of paper from the previous lessons' sword fights, in a bag or hat. One person draws a theme and reads it aloud. The other person "draws his sword" (figuratively) and quotes the verse that goes with that theme. Then they switch roles: the second person draws and the first person quotes the corresponding scripture. See the introduction under "Its Focus" for a complete explanation.

Paper Plate Lions

In the center of a paper plate, glue a black paper triangle for nose. Draw eyes or glue brown paper circles on for eyes. Color gold or brown around the bumpy rim of the plate as a mane. Fringe the edges with scissors. Cut thin strips of black paper for whiskers. Gently curl them by running them over the sharp edge of a pair of scissors. Glue the bottom edges of paper half-circles onto the top near the mane as ears. Discuss the reading of Daniel and talk about prayer.

Letter to God

> The child writes a letter to God, as if he were writing to a friend. He may make requests of God in the letter, as it is a kind of written prayer. Discuss prayer.

Prayer Notebook

> The child decorates the front of a small notebook, which will be his prayer notebook. He writes in it his prayer requests, and each lesson he can review it and write down the answers to those prayers.

Diorama

> Build a small scene of Elijah on Mt. Carmel. Use play dough or clay or small toy figures and other materials you might find around the house. Discuss prayer.

LESSON 11

Theme: Optimism

Verse: "All things work together for good to them who love God." Romans 8:28
(Write this verse on paper swords, one for each child. Older children can write it themselves.)

Reading 1:   II Kings 6:8-23—Elisha's Servant is Worried

Questions:

- Do you ever worry?
- Do you know anyone who is worried all the time?
- What does worry do for people?
- Who has the power to make things work out for good?
- Do things work out right away or does it sometimes take awhile? What do you think about that?

Reading 2:   Numbers 13:16-4:4—Twelve Spies

Reading 3:   Matthew 14:22-33—Peter Walks on Water

Reading 4:   II Kings 4:1-7—The Widow's Oil

Reading 5:   Acts 16:16-35—Paul and Silas in Jail

Activities

Sword Fight

Write the theme for this lesson on a slip of paper. Place that slip of paper, along with the slips of paper from the previous lessons' sword fights, in a bag or hat. One person draws a theme and reads it aloud. The other person "draws his sword" (figuratively) and quotes the verse that goes with that theme. Then they switch roles: the second person draws and the first person quotes the corresponding scripture. See the introduction under "Its Focus" for a complete explanation.

Drawing Eyes

Practice drawing eyes using the series of drawings below as a pattern. Then draw a face. Discuss Reading 1.

Paper Cup Chariot

Use three paper cups for each chariot. Cut out the bottom circles from two of the cups. Cut the third cup in half lengthwise. Use one of the halves lying sideways as the chariot. With paper fasteners (brads), attach the two circles on each side of the chariot as wheels. Discuss Reading 1.

Handprint Angels

In the middle of a piece of paper, draw a triangle
with its point at the top, and draw a circle atop
the point. The circle is the head of the angel.
The triangle is the body. Paint palms with
tempera or other water based paint. While
paint is still wet, press palms to the paper, one on
each side of the triangle to be angel wings.

Sinking/Floating

Fill a sink or bucket or tub or pan with water. Let
children gather items from the yard and house
to experiment with. They drop items one at a
time into the water to see which floats and which
sinks. How can a heavy ship float? Discuss
Reading 3. Discuss optimism.

Coil Pots

With clay or play dough, make a round disk
shape to be the base of the pot. Then make long
"snakes" by rolling the clay between your palms.
Coil the "snakes" around in a circle on the outer
edge of the base. Build one coil upon another
until you have a pot shape. Smooth the sides.
Discuss Reading 4.

LESSON 12

Theme: Harvest and Thanksgiving

Verse: "Give thanks to the Lord, for he is good." Psalm 136:1
(Write this verse on paper swords, one for each child. Older children can write it themselves.)

Reading 1: Ruth 2—Ruth Gathers Grain

Questions:
- What is harvest?
- Why do you think harvest is a time when people think about being thankful?
- Can we always find something to be thankful for, even when we are having problems?
- Why is it important to be thankful?
- Name some things you are thankful for.
- How can we show thankfulness?

Reading 2: Exodus 16—God Sends Manna

Reading 3: Genesis 18:1-15—Abraham Shares Food with Strangers

Reading 4: Psalm 106—A Psalm of Thanksgiving

Reading 5: Psalm 136—A Psalm of Thanksgiving

Activities

Sword Fight

Write the theme for this lesson on a slip of paper. Place that slip of paper, along with the slips of paper from the previous lessons' sword fights, in a bag or hat. One person draws a theme and reads it aloud. The other person "draws his sword" (figuratively) and quotes the verse that goes with that theme. Then they switch roles: the second person draws and the first person quotes the corresponding scripture. See the introduction under "Its Focus" for a complete explanation.

Grains in the Kitchen

Gather different types of grains. At home, look for them in the kitchen. In a classroom setting, bring a variety of grains. Oats, wheat flour, wheat germ, rice, barley, corn, cornmeal, puffed wheat, rice, and other cereal, etc. Compare them. Get a boxed breakfast cereal that has flakes made of different grains, try one kind of flake at a time and see if you can taste a difference. Discuss Reading 1 and gratitude.

Pasta Mosaic

With different shapes of pasta (and colors, if available), the child makes a mosaic picture. It can be of something real, or it can be simply a design. He glues the pasta shapes onto construction paper or cardboard to make this picture. Discuss Reading 2 and gratitude.

Thanksgiving's History

Each person tells what he knows about the history of Thanksgiving in the United States. Read a book or encyclopedia article about it if you wish. Then go to the book *The Light and the Glory* by Marshall and Manuel. Read from the middle of page 135 to almost the end of page 136. Is there a difference?

Cornucopia

Make a cornucopia centerpiece by rolling a large piece of brown construction paper into a cone shape. Staple or tape it together. Set it on its side and arrange small fruits and vegetables so they are spilling out.

Or: Make paper fruits and vegetables to go into the cornucopia.

- Make a carrot by rolling a tight, small cone of orange paper.
- Make an apple by folding a 6"x7" piece of red paper in half horizontally. Cut through both thicknesses from the fold to within ½" of the edge every ½ inch. Open it up and bring the 7" edges together to overlap. Staple or tape. Then curve the sides around and tape or staple.
- Make a pumpkin the same way as the apple, but use orange paper and make it a bit larger.
- Make decorative grain by cutting yellow paper into 1" strips. Cut one end into a fringe about 6" long.
- Green strips ¼" wide can be curled by gently running the sharp edge of scissors over it. Add these to the arrangement.

Ball Toss Scripture Tag

Children stand in a circle. Toss a large ball around the circle at random. Whoever catches the ball says the memory verse and then tosses it to another person. Make sure everyone gets a chance to catch and toss the ball.

LESSON 13

Theme: Patience

Verse: "There is a time for everything."
Ecclesiastes 3:1
(Write this verse on paper swords, one for each
child. Older children can write it themselves.)

Reading 1:   Ecclesiastes 3:1-8

Questions:

- What is patience?
- Name some times that it is hard to be patient.
- Why would God want us to be patient?
- Are there ever times when people need to be patient with you?

Reading 2:   Luke 5:1-10—The Disciples Fish all Night

Reading 3:   Genesis 29:16-30—Jacob Works to Marry Rachel

Reading 4:   Exodus 5-11—Moses Tries to Convince Pharaoh

Reading 5:   Luke 2:41-52—Jesus, the Carpenter, waits until he is grown to begin his ministry

Activities

Sword Fight

Write the theme for this lesson on a slip of paper. Place that slip of paper, along with the slips of paper from the previous lessons' sword fights, in a bag or hat. One person draws a theme and reads it aloud. The other person "draws his sword" (figuratively) and quotes the verse that goes with that theme. Then they switch roles: the second person draws and the first person quotes the corresponding scripture. See the introduction under "Its Focus" for a complete explanation.

The Sun's Movement

Place an object that will cast a shadow on a porch, sidewalk or driveway. Mark the shadow, or at least one side or point of it, with chalk. Leave the object there and check it every 10 or 15 minutes. Mark the shadow again. Observe and measure the distance the sun has moved over a period of time. You can also do this indoors on a table, counter or windowsill where the sun is shining in. Mark with tape. Discuss waiting and patience.

Paper Plate Clock

Use a drinking straw for the hands of the clock, cutting the straw into one shorter section and one longer section. With a paper fastener (brad) attach the two "hands" to the center of the paper plate. Mark off the numbers on the clock. Older children may want to use Roman numerals. If the children do not know how to tell time, you may want to work on this using this clock. Discuss patience.

Types of Clocks

From encyclopedias or other books, find out about different methods used in the past to tell time. Choose one or more to draw or try. Discuss patience.

Fishing

Cut paper fish from index cards or paper. Tape a paper clip to the back of each one. Write a number on each one. Make a fishing pole by tying one end of a string to a magnet and the other end to an unsharpened pencil, a stick or a dowel. Play this as a game by taking turns "fishing," and adding up points (the number on the fish) of all the fish each person catches. The person with the highest score wins. Older children may prefer to multiply their points. Discuss the patience that fishermen must have when they fish. Discuss Reading 2.

Fishing

Go fishing for real fish. Practice patience. Discuss Reading 2.

Television Show

Pretend you are putting on a television news show about Reading 4. Some children pretend to be reporters. Others are interviewed as Egyptians, and one could even be the Pharaoh, one could be Moses, some could be Pharaoh's magicians. Reporters ask questions about the situation in Egypt during the plagues. Discuss the patience that Moses had to have with Pharaoh.

LESSON 14

Theme: Empathy

Verse: "Rejoice with those who rejoice; mourn with those who mourn." Romans 12:15
(Write this verse on paper swords, one for each child. Older children can write it themselves.)

Reading 1:   John 11:1-44—Lazarus Dies, Jesus Weeps

Questions:

- Is it always easy to be happy when others are happy?
- Is it always easy to be sad when others are sad?
- Why would God want us to rejoice or mourn when others rejoice or mourn?
- Is there someone we need to rejoice with today?
- Is there someone we need to mourn with today?
- What are some ways we can show we are happy with someone?
- What are some ways we can show we are sad with someone?

Reading 2:   II Kings 6:1-7—Elisha and the Axe Head

Reading 3:   II Kings 4:8-36—Elisha Raises the Woman's Son

Reading 4:   Mark 2:1-12—Four Men with a Sick Friend

Reading 5:   Hebrews 4:14 ff —Jesus Knows How we Feel

Activities

Sword Fight

Write the theme for this lesson on a slip of paper. Place that slip of paper, along with the slips of paper from the previous lessons' sword fights, in a bag or hat. One person draws a theme and reads it aloud. The other person "draws his sword" (figuratively) and quotes the verse that goes with that theme. Then they switch roles: the second person draws and the first person quotes the corresponding scripture. See the introduction under "Its Focus" for a complete explanation.

Balloon Faces

Inflate balloons. With permanent markers, draw faces with different emotions on the balloons.

For older children or a family project, after balloons are inflated, make a mixture of flour and water the consistency of paste. Tear old newspaper into strips. Dip the strips of newspaper into the flour/water paste. Make sure the paper is saturated with the paste. Smooth off the excess paste by gently running the strip between your thumb and forefinger. Lay the strips across the balloon, covering the entire balloon. You can even mold nose, eyebrows, eyes and ears onto it. Let the newspaper (paper mache) dry and then stick a straight pin into the bottom to pop the balloon. The popped balloon does not need to come out, but you may pull it out the bottom if you wish. Paint the faces showing different emotions. Discuss rejoicing with those who rejoice and mourning with those who mourn.

Cardboard Axe

> Cut a piece of cardboard into an axe shape. Cover the blade section with foil.   Discuss Reading 2.

Pillows

> Cut fabric into 12" x 24" sections. (Use smaller sections for smaller pillows.) Fold the fabric with the right sides in. Sew along two sides and 3/4 of the third side. Turn the fabric right side out and stuff with polyester fiberfill (available at fabric stores or in sewing sections of some discount stores.) Discuss Reading 3 and/or 4. Perhaps give a pillow to someone who is sick at home in bed.

Float/Sink

> Cut two 4"x4" squares of foil. Roll one into a ball. Leave the other flat. Place both into water to see which one floats. Now see if you can mold the flat one into a boat shape that will float. What makes the difference between the one(s) that will float and the one(s) that will not float? Discuss Reading 2 and empathy.

Rejoice Party

> Make cupcakes and party hats. Decorate with balloons and streamers. Have a rejoice party. Each person tells something they can rejoice in or be thankful for. Dicsuss Readings 2, 3, and 4, and what those people could rejoice about.

LESSON 15

Theme: Obeying (Submitting to Authority)

Verse: "Children, obey your parents in the Lord, for this is right." Ephesians 6:1
(Write this verse on paper swords, one for each child. Older children can write it themselves.)

Reading 1:   Exodus 19:20-20:21
The Ten Commandments

Questions:

- Who are some of the people we should obey?
- Are there people we should not obey? Who?
- Why is it important to obey God?
- How do we know what God wants us to do?
- Talk about times you have obeyed. What were the consequences?
- Talk about times you have not obeyed. What were the consequences?

Reading 2:   Luke 7:1-10—The Centurion's Servant

Reading 3:   Mark 4:35-41—Jesus Stills the Storm

Reading 4:   Esther 4-5:8—Esther before the King

Reading 5:   Matthew 17:24-27—Jesus Pays the Tax

Activities

Sword Fight

Write the theme for this lesson on a slip of paper. Place that slip of paper, along with the slips of paper from the previous lessons' sword fights, in a bag or hat. One person draws a theme and reads it aloud. The other person "draws his sword" (figuratively) and quotes the verse that goes with that theme. Then they switch roles: the second person draws and the first person quotes the corresponding scripture. See the introduction under "Its Focus" for a complete explanation.

Making Change

Make numeral cards on 27 slips of paper or index cards by writing 0 on three cards, 1 on three cards, 2 on three cards and so on through the numeral 9. Write a decimal point on one card and a dollar sign on another. Make three different stacks of cards 1-9, and shuffle each stack, placing them face down in a row. Place the dollar sign to the left of the stacks and the decimal point between the first stack and the second stack.

Provide the children with several coins of each kind: pennies, nickels, dimes and quarters, plus some dollar bills. Play money can be used. One child turns over the top card on each stack. That is the price he must pay for pretend goods he is buying. He pays in bills, and another child must make change. Show him how to count the change back, starting with the price of the goods and adding the change on until he gets to the amount he was given. Discuss Reading 5 and obeying.

Coin Rubbing

Place a variety of coins under plain typing paper. Rub over them with a crayon, making their image on the paper. Discuss Reading 5 and obeying.

Designing Coins

Each person draws his own design of coin he would make if he were a coin designer. Discuss Reading 5 and obeying.

Play Dough Tablets

Using play dough (3 parts flour, 1 part salt, 1 part water) make "stone tablets" like Moses brought down from Mt. Sinai. If you make them large enough, write one or more of the laws on them. Discuss obeying.

Storm in a Jar

Use a jar with a lid. Fill it 3/4 full of water. Add a drop of dish detergent and 1/2 tsp. salt. Put the lid on the jar and shake it around in a circular motion. Then hold it still. You will see a funnel form and whirl around inside the jar. Discuss Reading 3 and obeying.

Scepters

Place a styrofoam ball on the end of a dowel to make a scepter. Decorate it with markers or glue and glitter or sequins and ribbons and plastic "jewels." Discuss Reading 4 and obeying.

LESSON 16

Theme: Generosity

Verse: "Each man should give what he has decided in his heart to give, not reluctantly or under compulsion, for God loves a cheerful giver." II Corinthians 9:7

(Write this verse on paper swords, one for each child. Older children can write it themselves.)

Reading 1: I Samuel 18:1-4—David and Jonathan

Questions:

- What does it mean to be generous?
- Why does God want us to be giving people?
- How was the person in the story generous?
- Tell about a time you were generous, or when someone was generous to you.

Reading 2: John 6:1-13—A Boy Shares Loaves and Fishes

Reading 3: Acts 9:36-43—Dorcas

Reading 4: Genesis 24:1-27—Rebekah Gives Water to Camels

Reading 5: Luke 6:38—Jesus' Promise about Giving

Activities

Sword Fight

Write the theme for this lesson on a slip of paper. Place that slip of paper, along with the slips of paper from the previous lessons' sword fights, in a bag or hat. One person draws a theme and reads it aloud. The other person "draws his sword" (figuratively) and quotes the verse that goes with that theme. Then they switch roles: the second person draws and the first person quotes the corresponding scripture. See the introduction under "Its Focus" for a complete explanation.

Sack Vests

Cut a paper grocery sack vertically from top to bottom in the center of one of its wide sides. From that vertical cut, cut a circle in the bottom of the sack large enough to fit around the child's neck. Cut arm holes in the sides of the sack. Decorate with markers, crayons or paint, or by gluing on rick-rack, ribbons and other decorations. Discuss Reading 1.

Option: Do as above, but use old pillowcases.

Orange Tea Mix

Mix one 18 oz. jar of orange breakfast drink mix, ¾ c. sugar, ½ c. presweetened lemonade mix, 1/2 c. instant decaffeinated tea, one 3 oz. package orange gelatin 2½ tsp. cinnamon, and ½ tsp. ground cloves. Divide the mixture into small jars or locking plastic bags. Put bows or ribbons on them and give them to someone. Discuss generosity.

Get Well Card

Fold paper in half. Make a get well card for someone who is sick. Mail it or take it to them. Discuss Reading 3.

Sewing Cards

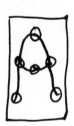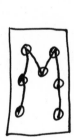

Use 3"x5" index cards. Give each child the same number of cards as there are letters in his first name. The child spells his first name, writing one letter on each card large enough to fill the card. Now, using a hole puncher, punch evenly spaced holes in each card along the lines of each letter. Using blunt-tipped sewing needles (used for sewing with yarn) and different colors of yarn, the child sews through the letters of each card. Discuss Reading 3.

Camel Shadows

> Project a bright light source (like a slide projector or bright lamp) onto a wall. With hands, try to make a camel shadow on the wall. It may take several people working together to make the camel and his hump. Discuss Reading 4.

Braided Belts

> For each belt, cut strips of cloth 1" wide and 2 yards long. Show children how to braid the strips. If they are too long to work with easily, roll each strip onto a pencil, or upon itself and secure with rubber band, letting out more fabric as it is needed. Discuss Reading 1.

LESSON 17

Theme: The Christmas Story

Verse: "God so loved the world that he sent his one and only Son." John 3:16
(Write this verse on paper swords, one for each child. Older children can write it themselves.)

Reading 1: Luke 1:26-38—Gabriel Announces Jesus' Birth

Questions:

- Why did God send Jesus as a baby?
- Why do you think he chose Mary?
- When you think of Jesus being a real baby, a real boy, a real man, what does that tell you about God?
- Do you think Jesus made choices to be the way he was?

Reading 2: Matthew 1:18-25—Joseph Finds Out

Reading 3: Luke 2:1-7—Jesus is Born

Reading 4: Luke 2:8-20—Shepherds Visit

Reading 5: Matthew 2:1-12—Wise Men Visit

Activities

Sword Fight

Write the theme for this Lesson on a slip of paper. Place that slip of paper, along with the slips of paper from the previous lesson s' sword fights, in a bag or hat. One person draws a theme and reads it aloud. The other person "draws his sword" (figuratively) and quotes the verse that goes with that theme. Then they switch roles: the second person draws and the first person quotes the corresponding scripture. See the introduction under "Its Focus" for a complete explanation.

A Tasty Gift

Bake cookies to take as a gift to someone. Wrap them in a basket or box and give them. Discuss the wise men and their gifts as well as the greatest gift of God's Son.

A Creche

Make figures of Mary, Joseph, wise men, and shepherds using clothespins. Draw faces on them using markers. Use bits of cloth to glue on or wrap around them as clothes. Glue on yarn or string for hair. Make a manger out of a box or bottle top, and make a baby with play dough.

Nativity Play

With one person as narrator reading from all the readings above, the children enact the nativity. This can be practiced and performed for another group of children, or parents, or neighborhood, if you want.

Caroling

Choose some older people, or new people who have moved into the neighborhood, or shut-ins, and go to their houses to sing Christmas carols to them.

Angel Wreath

Use cookie cutters shaped like angels, or show the children how to draw angels using triangles and circles. Children use cookie cutters as stencils and draw around them, or draw their own angels out of triangles and circles. Then cut them out and arrange them in a circle to form a wreath. Glue them together and hang the wreath.

LESSON 18

Theme: First Things First (Setting Priorities)

Verse: "Seek first God's kingdom and his righteousness
                  and all you need will be given to you."
                  Matthew 6:33
                  (Write this verse on paper swords, one for each
                  child. Older children can do this themselves.)

Reading 1:   Genesis 19:12-26—Lot's Wife

Questions:

- How do you decide what is most important to do?

- What is God's promise if we put first things first?

- Can you think of a time when you might have to choose between what God wants and what you or someone else wants?

- Is it always easy to put first things first?

Reading 2:   Genesis 25:19-34—Esau Sells his Birthright

Reading 3:   Daniel 3—The Fiery Furnace

Reading 4:   Matthew 6:19-21—Treasures in Heaven

Reading 5:   II Chronicles 1:6-12—Solomon Asks for Wisdom

Activities

Sword Fight

Write the theme for this Lesson on a slip of paper. Place that slip of paper, along with the slips of paper from the previous Lessons' sword fights, in a bag or hat. One person draws a theme and reads it aloud. The other person "draws his sword" (figuratively) and quotes the verse that goes with that theme. Then they switch roles: the second person draws and the first person quotes the corresponding scripture. See the introduction under "Its Focus" for a complete explanation.

Salt Play Dough

Make salt dough by mixing 3 c. flour, 1 c. salt, and 1 c. water. Make figures with it. Discuss Reading 1.

Lentil Soup

Make lentil soup. Bring to a boil 3½ c. of water, 1 c. lentils, 2 tsp. beef bouillon, 2 tsp. instant minced onions, ¼ tsp. pepper, 1 bay leaf, and salt to taste. Add one small can of tomatoes, if desired. Turn heat to low and simmer for 1½ to 2 hours. Eat and discuss Reading 2.

"Radio Drama"

Record the story of the fiery furnace on audio cassette, acting it out for listening purposes. You may have a narrator if you wish. Add sound effects as you are recording it. Crinkling cellophane makes a good fire sound. Discuss Reading 3.

Fire Drill

Discuss how to get out of your house or building in case of fire. Have a fire drill. Discuss Reading 3.

Wisdom Box

Each person needs a small box (like the kind checks come in, or a file card box), and index cards or slips of paper. Write one Proverb (from the book of Proverbs) on each card and place the cards in the box. Decorate the "wisdom box." Keep it or give it as a gift to someone special. Discuss Reading 5.

LESSON 19

Theme: Being Considerate

Verse: "Each of you should look not only to his own interests, but also to the interests of others." Philippians 2:4
(Write this verse on paper swords, one for each child. Older children can write it themselves.)

Reading 1: John 13:1-9—Jesus Washes his Disciples' Feet

Questions:

- How can you be considerate of others?
- Tell about a time you were considerate of someone, or when someone was considerate of you.
- Who was considerate in the story?
- Why is it important to be considerate?
- Is it always easy to be considerate?

Reading 2: Luke 10:25-37—The Good Samaritan

Reading 3: Mark 10:13-16—Jesus and the Children

Reading 4: II Samuel 9—David and Mephibosheth

Reading 5: Matthew 25:31-46—"If you've done it to the least of these . . ."

Activities

Sword Fight

Write the theme for this lesson on a slip of paper. Place that slip of paper, along with the slips of paper from the previous lesson s' sword fights, in a bag or hat. One person draws a theme and reads it aloud. The other person "draws his sword" (figuratively) and quotes the verse that goes with that theme. Then they switch roles: the second person draws and the first person quotes the corresponding scripture. See the introduction under "Its Focus" for a complete explanation.

Washing Feet

Get a large pan of water and a towel and wash each others' feet. Discuss Reading 1.

Serve Snacks

The children prepare and serve snacks. This can be as simple as peanut butter on crackers with juice, or it can include baking cookies or bread sticks and making lemonade. Discuss being a servant, Reading 1, and being considerate.

First Aid

Use a good first aid book, or invite a nurse or doctor to talk to the children. Find out how to do simple first aid procedures and practice them. Discuss Reading 2.

Diorama of the Good Samaritan

Make a model of the road where the injured man was, and place figures around to represent the story. This can be as simple or fancy as you want. Figures can be play dough figures you have made, or toy figures, or clothespins made into figures. Discuss the story, and let children tell it using the diorama.

Puppets

Make puppets out of plastic spoons. Draw features on with permanent markers. Glue on hair. Tie or glue fabric on for clothes. Make one puppet for each character in the Good Samaritan story. Then children practice and put on a puppet show using the puppets.

LESSON 20

Theme: Pride and Stubborness

Verse: "Pride goes before destruction and a haughty
                  spirit before a fall." Proverbs 16:18
                  (Write this verse on paper swords, one for each
                  child. Older children can write it themselves.)

Reading 1:   Daniel 4:28-37—Nebuchadnezzar Eats Grass

Questions:
                  • What is pride?
                  • Who was proud in the story?
                  • Why is this kind of pride bad?
                  • Is there a good kind of pride?
                  • Read James 4:6. What does God do about the
                     proud?

Reading 2:   Esther 5:9-6:11—Proud Haman

Reading 3:   Daniel 5—Handwriting on the Wall

Reading 4:   Numbers 22:1-35—Balaam and his Donkey

Reading 5:   II Samuel 14:25-15:16 and 18:1-15—Absalom

Activities

Sword Fight

Write the theme for this lesson on a slip of paper. Place that slip of paper, along with the slips of paper from the previous lessons' sword fights, in a bag or hat. One person draws a theme and reads it aloud. The other person "draws his sword" (figuratively) and quotes the verse that goes with that theme. Then they switch roles: the second draws and the first person quotes the corresponding scripture.

Grasses we Eat

In a kitchen, go on a hunt to find all the things that are made from grains (grasses). Besides bread, look for pastas, flours, cereals, oats. If you want to explore further, look in an encyclopedia or other book, and find out what these grasses look like as they are growing. Using a piece of paper for each grain, draw a picture of each one at the top. List some of the things that are made from that grain underneath. Discuss Reading 1 and pride.

Hand Shadows

Project a bright light onto a wall, using a slide projector or other bright lamp. Children make different hand shadows on the wall. Act out the story of the handwriting on the wall. Discuss Reading 3 and pride.

Name Shadows

Fold a large piece of construction paper in half lengthwise. Draw a ½" border across the fold side. This is the base line. The child writes (cursive or printing) his name on that line in large letters. Then he cuts through both thicknesses of paper along the baseline and around the outline of each letter, leaving the letters attached to the baseline at the bottom. Do not cut on the fold. Cut out the center areas of the letters that need it. Then fold out the name and stand it up with its shadow as the prop. Discuss Reading 3 and pride.

Donkey Puppets

Use a paper or styrofoam cup as the donkey's head. Glue or tape triangle paper ears on the side of the cup toward the rim, and glue a triangle nose on the bottom of the cup. Draw eyes on, or glue on paper circles or craft eyes. The child's hand fits inside the cup to make it a puppet. Discuss Reading 4 and pride.

Absalom Hair

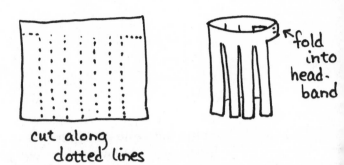

cut along
dotted lines

Cut strips up to within one inch of the top of a large piece of black construction paper. Place it around the child's head as a headband. If it does not reach all the way around, cut a band of paper one inch wide to staple to the top of the construction paper. It should be long enough to complete the circle around the child's head like a headband. Cut off any strips that get in the way of the child's face. Wear as hair. Discuss Reading 5 and pride.

LESSON 21

Theme: Selflessness

Verse: "Do nothing out of selfish ambition or vain conceit, but in humility consider others better than yourselves." Philippians 2:3
(Write this verse on paper swords, one for each child. Older children can write it themselves.)

Reading 1:   Luke 21:1-4—The Widow Gives the Mite

Questions:

- What is the opposite of being selfish?
- How can we be selfless?
- Who was selfless in the story? How?
- Tell about someone you know who was selfless.
- Is it easy to be selfless?

Reading 2:   Luke 9:46-48—Disciples Argue

Reading 3:   Luke 16:19-31—Rich Man and Lazarus

Reading 4:   I Samuel 25:1-42—Nabal and Abigail

Reading 5:   Ruth 1:1-19—Ruth goes with Naomi

Activities

Sword Fight

Write the theme for this lesson on a slip of paper. Place that slip of paper, along with the slips of paper from the previous lessons' sword fights, in a bag or hat. One person draws a theme and reads it aloud. The other person "draws his sword" (figuratively) and quotes the verse that goes with that theme. Then they switch roles: the second person draws and the first person quotes the corresponding scripture. See the introduction under "Its Focus" for a complete explanation.

Banks

Make money banks out of margarine tubs. Cut slits in the lids so that coins will fit in. Cut different colors of contact paper into small triangles and circles and rectangles and squares, and put them on the lid and sides of the margarine tubs to decorate them. Discuss Reading 1. Discuss being selfless.

Collection of Money

Collect money and give it to someone who needs it, or use it to buy something for someone in need, or someone who is sick. Discuss Reading 1. Discuss selflessness.

Musical Chairs

Play musical chairs. Set out one less chair than there are people. One person is in charge of the music. When this person turns on the music, the others march around the chairs. When the music is turned off, everyone tries to sit in a chair as quickly as possible. The person who ends up without a chair is out. One chair is removed, and the game is repeated until only one person is left. That person is the winner. Discuss games, including sports. Can sports games be selfless? How? Is there a way you could change the game musical chairs to be more selfless?

Abigail Snack

Make raisin cakes. Heat ¼ c. sugar, 1 Tbs. cornstarch, 1 c. water and 2 c. raisins in a pan on the stove. When it is thick, remove it from the heat and let it cool. Cream ½ c. margarine and 1 c. brown sugar together. Stir in a mixture of 1½ c. flour, ½ tsp. soda and ½ tsp. salt. Now stir in 1 ½ c. oats and 1 Tbs. water. Press one half of this mixture into a 13"x9" baking pan. Spread the raisin mixture over it. On top, spread the rest of the flour/oat mixture. Bake at 350° for 35 minutes. Discuss Reading 4, and selflessness.

Follow the Leader

Play follow the leader by choosing one person to lead. The others follow wherever he leads and does what he does. Discuss Reading 5 and selflessness. Can a leader be selfless? How?

LESSON 22

Theme: Accepting Others

Verse: "In humility consider others better than your-self." Philippians 2:3
(Write this verse on paper swords, one for each child. Older children can write it themselves.)

Reading 1:   Mark 10:46-52—Blind Bartimaeus

Questions:

- How are people different from each other?
- Do you know anyone with a handicap?
- How can you be a friend to them?
- Who was different in the story?
- Why do you think God wants us to accept others?
- How does it feel not to be accepted?
- How does it feel to be accepted?

Reading 2:   Luke 19:1-10—Jesus and Zacchaeus

Reading 3:   Acts 10—Peter and Cornelius

Reading 4:   John 4:1-42—The Woman at the Well

Reading 5:   Joshua 2—Rahab and the Spies

Activities

Sword Fight

Write the theme for this lesson on a slip of paper. Place that slip of paper, along with the slips of paper from the previous lesson s' sword fights, in a bag or hat. One person draws a theme and reads it aloud. The other person "draws his sword" (figuratively) and quotes the verse that goes with that theme. Then they switch roles: the second person draws and the first person quotes the corresponding scripture. See the introduction under "Its Focus" for a complete explanation.

Blindfolded Partners

Children choose partners. Blindfold one of them. Tell them where they are to go, either through certain rooms, or around a yard. The child without the blindfold leads his partner around, telling him where to turn and step up or down. After they have finished their walk, they switch places. The blindfolded partner now becomes the leader, and the leader is blindfolded. Give them a different path to follow. Discuss Reading 1 and people with handicaps. Discuss accepting others.

Stilts

Cut a wood 4"x4" into 4" lengths. Use two of these cubes for each pair of stilts. Saw a groove around each end of the cube about 1/2" from the end. Tie a piece of string around each groove. To each of these strings, tie a length of string equal to the distance from the floor to the child's wrist. Tie the ends of the long strings of one block together. Tie the ends of the long strings of the other block together. The child stands on the blocks and holds onto the long strings, keeping the strings taut as he walks. Discuss Reading 2 and accepting others.

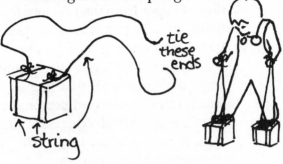

tie these ends

string

Heights

Give each child a strip of adding machine tape that is taller than he is. Using markers and crayons (and stickers—optional), each child decorates his strip of paper to be hung vertically. After it is decorated, tape it to the wall and mark the child's height on it. Then let older children use a ruler or measuring tape and measure how tall they are in inches. Discuss Reading 2 and accepting others.

Body Proportions

Are you short-waisted or long-waisted or neither? Try this: put your elbows to your side and raise your lower arms up. If your elbows come above your waist, you are long-waisted. If your elbows come below your waist, you are short-waisted. If your elbows come exactly to your waist, you are neither.

Try this: put your foot to your forearm with your heal at your elbow. Where do your toes come to? Is this true with everyone?

Try this: draw a face with eyes, ears, nose and mouth. Where did you put the ears? How large are they? Look carefully at people's ears. Tops of ears are usually even with their eyes. The bottoms are usually even with their upper lip. Discuss accepting others.

Hide and Go Seek

Play hide and go seek. One person closes his eyes and counts to an agreed upon number. The others hide. When the seeker finishes counting, he calls, "Ready or not, here I come." Then he tries to find the others. Discuss Reading 5 and accepting others.

LESSON 23

Theme: Encouraging Others

Verse: "Let us consider how we may spur one another on toward love and good deeds."   Hebrews 20:24
(Write this verse on paper swords, one for each child. Older children can write it themselves.)

Reading 1:   Numbers 13:26-14:9—Joshua and Caleb—Faith Encourages

Questions:

- Have you ever been discouraged—you just want to give up?
- Tell of a time when someone encouraged you.
- What encourages you?
- How can we encourage others?
- Who encouraged someone in our story?
- Why do you suppose God wants us to be encouragers?

Reading 2:   Genesis 50:15-21—Joseph Forgives—Forgiving Encourages

Reading 3:   Ruth 2—Boaz Leaves Grain—Sharing Encourages

Reading 4:   John 1:35-49—Jesus Encourages Peter and Nathaniel—Saying Nice Things about others Encourages

Reading 5:   Matthew 9:9-12—Jesus is Kind to Matthew—Being Kind Encourages

Activities

Sword Fight

Write the theme for this lesson on a slip of paper. Place that slip of paper, along with the slips of paper from the previous lessons' sword fights, in a bag or hat. One person draws a theme and reads it aloud. The other person "draws his sword" (figuratively) and quotes the verse that goes with that theme. Then they switch roles: the second person draws and the first person quotes the corresponding scripture. See the introduction under "Its Focus" for a complete explanation.

Diorama of Canaan

Using clay or play dough (3 c. flour, 1 c. salt, 1 c. water) and a map of Canaan (found in many Bibles), make a map of Canaan complete with mountains and rivers and plains. Discuss Reading 1 and encouraging others.

Tricky Spyglass

Use a cardboard tube from a paper towel roll. Place it to your left eye as if looking through a spyglass or telescope, but keep both eyes open. Now place your right hand up, resting against the side of the tube, palm side toward your face. Slowly pull your hand toward you or extend it away from you until you see a hole in your hand. The child may color his tube with crayons or markers. Discuss Reading 1 and encouraging others.

Finger Puppets

With washable markers, draw faces on fingers. If you have an old pair of gloves, the faces can be drawn on the fingers of the gloves. Prepare a puppet show about Reading 1 or 2. Talk about encouraging others.

Name Meanings

Get a name book that tells meanings of names. One of these is *The Name Book* by Dorothea Austin, published by Bethany House. On a piece of construction paper, the child writes his name as if making a plaque. He may color it or design it as he wishes. Under his name, he writes the meaning. Discuss Reading 4, and encouraging others.

Collect Food or Clothes

Find someone who needs food or clothes and collect food or clothes to give to them. Discuss Reading 3, and encouraging others.

LESSON 24

Theme: Choosing Friends

Verse: "A friend loves at all times." Proverbs 17:17
                 (Write this verse on paper swords, one for each
                 child. Older children can write it themselves.)

Reading 1:   I Samuel 20—Jonathan Warns David

Questions:
                 • What makes a good friend?

                 • How do you choose your friends?

                 • Who were friends in the story? Was it a good
                   choice of friends or a bad choice?

                 • What is the danger of having bad friends?

                 • Why do we need good friends?

                 • Tell about some of your best friends.

Reading 2:   Acts 8:26-40—Philip and the Eunuch (discuss
                 strangers)

Reading 3:   Acts 16:11-15—Paul and Lydia

Reading 4:   John 21:1-14—Jesus Prepares Breakfast

Reading 5:   Judges 16:1-22—Samson and Delilah (the wrong
                 kind of friends)

Activities

Sword Fight

Write the theme for this lesson on a slip of paper. Place that slip of paper, along with the slips of paper from the previous lessons' sword fights, in a bag or hat. One person draws a theme and reads it aloud. The other person "draws his sword" (figuratively) and quotes the verse that goes with that theme. Then they switch roles: the seconds person draws and the first person quotes the corresponding scripture. See the introduction under "Its Focus" for a complete explanation.

Pictures

Take photographs of children with their friends. When they are developed, glue or tape the pictures to squares of construction paper to make a frame. Give one photo to each child in the picture. Discuss one of the readings and choosing friends.

Tie-dye Purple

Use purple dye that is intended for use in tie-dye (available at craft stores). Follow the directions on the dye to prepare the dye and dye the fabric. Dye tee-shirts or bandana-sized squares of muslin by tyeing the fabric or bunching it up and wrapping it with rubber bands. You may wish to dip only small sections of the fabric into the dye. Let it dry. Wear it as tee-shirt or bandana, or give it to a friend. Discuss Reading 3 and choosing friends.

Dyed Wind Flags

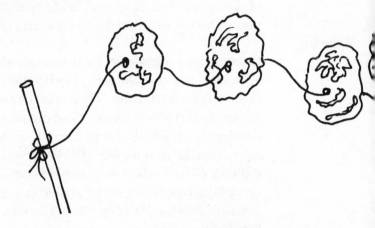

Fill three coffee cups one-third full with rubbing alcohol. Drip red food coloring in one cup, yellow food coloring in another cup, and blue food coloring in the third cup. Take several coffee filters for drip coffee makers (like Mr. Coffee) and fold each one at random. Dip parts of each filter very briefly into the different colors of dye. Lay them on newspaper to dry. They will dry quickly. Then thread a 36" or longer string into a needle used for sewing with yarn. Tie the end of the string. Run the string through the center of one coffee filter all the way to the knot. Tie another knot on the other side of the filter. Tie another knot about 5" from this knot. Run the string through the next filter all the way to that knot. Tie another knot on the other side to hold it in place. Tie another knot about 5" from this knot. Continue to add filters to the string in this way, holding each in place with a knot. Then tie the end to a porch or rail or post outside to blow in the breeze. Discuss Reading 3, and choosing friends.

Breakfast

Make scrambled eggs and toast and orange juice. Discuss Reading 4 and choosing friends.

Weaving

Cut ten strips of fabric ten inches long and about ½" wide. Lay out one strip horizontally. Tie eight strips onto this one. Then take the remaining strips and weave them in and out across the first strips. Go over the first strip, under the next, over the next and so on. When you get to the end of that row, use another strip for the next row, except this time go under the ones you went over before, and go over the strips you went under. Reverse this every time you start a new row. When you are finished, cut off excess fabric. Discuss Reading 5 and choosing friends.

LESSON 25

Theme: Respect for Others

Verse: "In humility consider others better than your-
                  self." Philippians 2:3
                  (Write this verse on paper swords, one for each
                  child. Older children can write it themselves.)

Reading 1:   Exodus 3:1-6—Moses and the Burning Bush
                  (respect for God)

Questions:

- What is respect?
- Who was respectful in the story?
- How did he show respect?
- Who should you be respectful to?
- Can you respect someone even if you don't
  like them?
- How can you show respect?
- Tell of a time when you were respectful or
  someone was respectful to you.

Reading 2:   I Samuel 24—David does not kill Saul
                  (respect for position)

Reading 3:   Daniel 2—Daniel before the Commander
                  (notice how politely and respectfully he speaks)

Reading 4:   Luke 2:41-52—Jesus Respects Mary and Jo-
                  seph

Reading 5:   Ruth 4:1-12 Boaz Respects the Elders and their
                  Tradition

Activities

Sword Fight

Write the theme for this lesson on a slip of paper. Place that slip of paper, along with the slips of paper from the previous lessons' sword fights, in a bag or hat. One person draws a theme and reads it aloud. The other person "draws his sword" (figuratively) and quotes the verse that goes with that theme. Then they switch roles: the second person draws and the first person quotes the corresponding scripture. See introduction under "Its Focus" for a complete explanation.

Nature Walk

Take a walk and notice seasonal changes, especially in the bushes. Imagine what it would have been like to see a bush burning, but not burning up. Discuss Reading 1 and respect.

Story in a Cave

Make a cave using cardboard boxes and package tape. Discuss Reading 2 and respect.

Cave Diorama

Use play dough or clay to make a mountain with a cave or several caves. If you make several caves, try to connect them. Discuss Reading 2 and respect.

Poster Montage

Children cut out pictures of many different kinds of people from magazines and catalogues. Glue them on a piece of posterboard. Discuss respect.

Carpentry

Provide wood and nails (and saws if you want). Let the children use their imaginations to build something. They can either decide together on one large thing to build with each other, or each one can build something smaller. Discuss Reading 4 and Jesus' childhood in Joseph's carpenter shop. Discuss respect.

LESSON 26

Theme: Wisdom

Verse: "Wisdom is more precious than rubies, and nothing you desire can compare with her." Proverbs 8:11

(Write this verse on paper swords, one for each child. Older children can write it themselves.)

Reading 1: Selections from Proverbs 1:1-4:27, 6:6-19, James 1:5, and James 3:13-17

Questions:

- How can you tell someone is wise?

- How do you become wise?

- What is the difference between wisdom and knowledge?

- Can someone know a lot and still not be wise? How?

- Can someone be wise and not know a lot? How?

- Tell of someone you know who is wise.

- Why does God want us to be wise?

Reading 2: II Chronicles 1—Solomon asks for Wisdom

Reading 3: Matthew 13:44-58 —Jesus' Wisdom

Reading 4: Matthew 25:1-13—Wise and Foolish Young Women

Reading 5: Genesis 41—Joseph Chosen to be a Ruler

Activities

Sword Fight

Write the theme for this lesson on a slip of
paper. Place that slip of paper, along with the
slips of paper from the previous lessons' sword
fights, in a bag or hat. One person draws a
theme and reads it aloud. The other person
"draws his sword" (figuratively) and quotes the
verse that goes with that theme. Then they
switch roles: the second person draws and the
first person quotes the corresponding scripture.

Lanterns

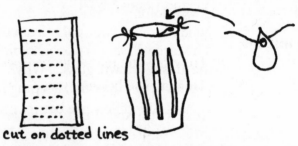

cut on dotted lines

Make "lanterns" by folding construction paper
in half vertically. Cut the paper every ½"
through both thicknesses from the fold to within
½" of the edge. Now unfold the paper and roll
it into a cylinder with the slits running vertically.
Staple the ends together. Cut out a yellow or
orange flame about 3"x2". With a hole puncher,
punch a hole in the top of the flame, and two
holes in the top of the lantern on opposite sides.
Tie one end of a string through one of the holes
in the lantern. Run the loose end through the
flame and then through the other hole in the
lantern. Tie it there. Cut a 1"x10" strip of
construction paper for the handle of the lantern. Staple it to the top. (See illustration on next
page.) Discuss Reading 4 and wisdom.

Wisdom vs. Knowledge

cut on dotted lines

hold over light
bulb

Do these experiments. First, fill a clear glass halfway with water. Place an index card or piece of cardboard over the top of the glass and hold it on with your palm. Turn the glass upside down, holding the index card on the glass. Now gently remove your palm from the index card. The card will stay in place, holding the water in the upside down glass. Why? Air pressure pushes up on the card, keeping it from falling.

Next, cut a spiral out of paper and attach a thread or string to the center of the spiral, letting it dangle downward. Now hold the spiral over a light bulb in a lamp that is turned on. What happens to the spiral? What does that tell you about heat? It rises. After these two experiments, discuss the difference between wisdom and knowledge.

Calendars

On paper, make a grid of five rows and seven columns, as on a calendar. Photocopy these so that the child has twelve to work with. He makes a calendar by stapling or tying (with ribbon through holes punched in the top) the pages together. Using a current calendar as a pattern, he can number the squares, write in the names of each month, and decorate each page of his calendar. Discuss Reading 4. Do we know exactly when Jesus will come back? What does this reading tell us about what is wise?

Treasures

Cut gem shapes out of construction paper, using different colors for the different gems: green for emeralds, red for rubies, yellow for topaz, blue for sapphires, purple for amethyst, white for pearls, and use waxed paper for diamonds. On each gem, write in permanent marker one of the characteristics of heavenly wisdom from James 3:17 (pure, peace loving, considerate, submissive, merciful, impartial, sincere). Cut a long piece of ribbon and glue each gem on the ribbon to hang on the wall, or punch holes in the tops and hang them on different lengths of string to a coat hanger to make a mobile. Discuss Reading 1 and/or Reading 3.

Collecting Litter

Go to a park or down a street and pick up litter and put it into trash bags. Discuss the wisdom of keeping our world clean. Do people of this world have wisdom? Recycling is wise. Keeping litter off the streets is wise. What are some things that most people do that are wise? What is the difference between the wisdom of the world and the wisdom that comes from God?

LESSON 27

Theme: Calm Spirit/Peace

Verse: "If it is possible, as far as it depends on you, live at peace with everyone." Romans 12:18

Reading 1:   I Samuel 16:14-23—Saul Listens to the Harp

Questions:

- What is peace?
- Tell about times when you feel peaceful.
- How can you live at peace with someone?
- Tell about the peace in the story.

Reading 2:   Matthew 6:25-34—Sermon on the Mount

Reading 3:   John 14:23-27—Jesus Talks about Peace

Reading 4:   Gen. 2:2,3 and Ex. 31:12-18—The Sabbath Day

Reading 5:   I Chronicles 22:2-19—Solomon and a Time of Peace

Activities

Sword Fight

Write the theme for this lesson on a slip of paper. Place that slip of paper, along with the slips of paper from the previous lessons' sword fights, in a bag or hat. One person draws a theme and reads it aloud. The other person "draws his sword" (figuratively) and quotes the verse that goes with that theme. Then they switch roles: the second person draws and the first person quotes the corresponding scripture. See introduction under "Its Focus" for a complete explanation.

Paper Lilies

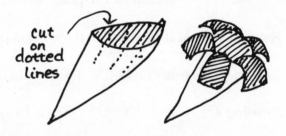

cut on dotted lines

Glue a piece of yellow or pink paper to a piece of white paper. With the colored piece of paper inside, make a cone and tape or staple it in place. Now cut from the outer, wide edge of the cone about 4" toward the narrow end. Cut three or four of these slits, evenly spaced around to make petals. Gently bend these petals out, showing the colored paper inside. Discuss Reading 2 and a peaceful, calm spirit.

Surface Tension

Fill a glass or cup with water. Rub a needle

between your fingers. Place it on a fork and gently lay the needle on top of the water, being careful not to get the needle wet. The surface tension of the water holds the needle up. Surface tension is made by molecules of water holding together to form a sort of skin. Discuss a different meaning of tension: stress, the opposite of peace. What causes tension? Is there anything we can do about it?

Water Temperature

Place ice in one jar of water. Boil some water. Pour it into another jar. Take the ice out of the ice water. Now drip a couple of drops of food coloring into each jar. What happens? Have you ever heard someone say they were boiling mad? Have you ever felt tension or stress or anger—like your feelings were swirling around inside you? Discuss peace.

A Peaceful Place

Take a walk in a park or on a nature trail, or find another peaceful spot to sit and talk. Close your eyes and just listen for a few minutes. Then talk about what makes this spot peaceful. Would there be times when this place would not be peaceful? Discuss what gives us peace. Discuss the purpose of the Sabbath Day.

Building a Temple

Read the Bible's description of the temple. As you read it, try to draw what you think it must have looked like. Then use blocks or boxes or other materials to build a model of the temple. Discuss Reading 5.

LESSON 28

Theme: Persistence

Verse: Let us not become weary in doing good, for . . . we will reap a harvest if we do not give up." Galatians 6:9

(Write this verse on paper swords, one for each child. Older children can write it themselves.)

Reading 1: Jeremiah 36—The King Burns Jeremiah's Scroll

Questions:
- What is persistence?
- Who was persistent in the reading?
- What does the verse mean? Talk about how it would relate to a farmer.
- Is it easy to be persistent? Why?
- Tell of a time when you were persistent.

Reading 2: Nehemiah 2:11-20, 4:1-23, 6:1-16
Rebuilding the Walls

Reading 3: Luke 18:1-8—The Persistent Widow

Reading 4: Acts 12:1-17—Peter Knocks at Rhoda's Door

Reading 5: Genesis 18:16-33—Abraham Asks God to Save Sodom

Activities:

Sword Fight

Write the theme for this lesson on a slip of paper. Place that slip of paper, along with the slips of paper from the previous lessons' sword fights, in a bag or hat. One person draws a theme and reads it aloud. The other person "draws his sword" (figuratively) and quotes the verse that goes with that theme. Then they switch roles: the second person draws and the first person quotes the corresponding scripture. See the introduction under "Its Focus" for a complete explanation.

Scrolls

Cut a piece of typing paper in half vertically. On this paper, the child rewrites one of the readings in his own words, or draws a picture (or sequence of pictures) to illustrate the story. If this takes more than one piece of paper, tape the paper together by their short ends to make a long strip. Tape each end of the strip to an unsharpened pencil. Roll the strip up onto the pencils, rolling each end toward the middle of the strip, so they meet in the middle to make a scroll. Discuss Reading 1 and persistence.

Knocking Game

Two players stand on opposite sides of a door. One of them knocks a rhythm. The other knocks, trying to copy the same rhythm. This continues until one player is not able to copy the rhythm. Another version of this can be played by having one player tap out the rhythm of a commonly known song, and the other player

trying to guess what song it is. Discuss Reading
4 and persistence.

Sugar Cube Wall

Make a city wall by gluing sugar cubes together.
Use small boxes or blocks or play dough build-
ings to put inside the city. Discuss Reading 2 and
persistence.

Whose Voice

One person is blindfolded. The others stand or
sit in different parts of the room. Each person,
one at a time, asks "Who am I?" The blindfolded
person tries to guess whose voice it is. To make
the game harder, each person can try to disguise
his voice, and/or the blindfolded person can
guess whether that person is standing or sitting
by listening to the direction the voice comes
from. Discuss Reading 4 and persistence.

Pudding

Make pudding from scratch. The constant
stirring will take persistence and patience. Mix
¾ c. sugar, ¼ c. flour, and ¼ tsp. salt in a pan.
Pour in 2 c. milk. Heat this, stirring constantly,
until it gets thick and bubbles. Remove it from
the heat. Beat 2 eggs well. Stir a spoonful of hot
pudding into the eggs, and then immediately
stir the eggs into the pan of pudding. Cook and
stir for 2 more minutes. Take it off of the heat
and add 2 Tbs. of margarine and 1 tsp. vanilla.
Discuss persistence and patience.

LESSON 29

Theme: Courage

Verse: "In God I trust; I will not be afraid." Psalm 56:11
(Write this verse on paper swords, one for each
child. Older children can write it themselves.)

Reading 1:   I Samuel 17—David and Goliath

Questions:

- Who was afraid in our reading?
- Who had courage in our reading?
- Describe what you think the setting would
  have been like.
- What would you have done in that situation?
- What are some things we might be afraid of?
- Tell about a fearful time when God took care
  of you.
- What are some things we can think of that will
  help us to have courage?

Reading 2:   Judges 6:36-7:22—Gideon

Reading 3:   I Samuel 10:9-25—King Saul

Reading 4:   Genesis 6:22-8:22—Noah on the Ark During
the Flood

Reading 5:   Genesis 28:10-17—Jacob's Dream

Activities

Sword Fight

Write the theme for this lesson on a slip of paper. Place that slip of paper, along with the slips of paper from the previous lessons' sword fights, in a bag or hat. One person draws a theme and reads it aloud. the other person "draws his sword" (figuratively) and quotes the verse that goes with that theme. Then they switch roles: the second person draws and the first person quotes the corresponding scripture. See the introduction under "Its Focus" for a complete explanation.

Stone Page Holders

Collect small pebbles or stones. Cut a piece of felt about 8" long and 2" wide. Glue the stones to each end. When dry, this page holder can be placed on an open book to keep the book open. This is helpful when the reader is using his hands for something else, such as cooking or writing, etc. Discuss Reading 1 and courage.

Paper Angels

Make a cone out of a white piece of typing paper. Tape or staple it in place. At the top (narrow) end of the cone, insert the handle of a white plastic spoon. With a permanent marker, make a face on the bowl of the spoon. Glue on yarn hair if you want. Now fold another piece of white typing paper accordion-style. Staple it in the middle and spread out the ends. Tape the middle to the back of the cone to make wings. Discuss Reading 5 and courage.

Act it Out

Act out the story of Gideon, Reading 2.

Animal Masks

Use large paper plates. Cut holes for eyes. Glue on features of construction paper. Curl paper for eyelashes and hair by rolling the paper on a drinking straw or pencil, or by gently pulling the paper across the sharp side of a pair of scissors. Another option is to use paint or markers to make the mask. Glue on paper or pipe cleaner whiskers. Discuss Reading 4 and courage.

Animal Cookies

Make animal cookies out of sugar cookie dough. Cut them out with cookie cutters, or mold them using plenty of flour to keep them from sticking to your hands. Features can be made out of red hots or cake decorations. Discuss Reading 4 and courage.

Dream Clouds Mobile

Cut cloud shapes out of white paper. On each cloud, the child writes or draws something that he would like to dream about. On one cloud, he draws an angel to represent Jacob's dream. Punch holes in the tops of the clouds, tie strings through them, and hand them from a clothes hanger. Discuss Reading 5 and courage.

LESSON 30

Theme: Easter

Verse: "He has risen!" Mark 16:6
(Write this verse on paper swords, one for each child. Older children can write it themselves.)

Reading 1: Matthew 21:7-11—The Triumphal Entry

Questions:

- Why did Jesus die?
- Why is it important that Jesus died?
- Why is it important that Jesus rose?
- Tell the story as if you had been there.
- Where is Jesus now?

Reading 2: Luke 22:7-20—The Last Supper

Reading 3: Luke 22:39-43—Garden of Gethsemane

Reading 4: John 19:17-42—Calvary

Reading 5: John 20:1-18—Resurrection

Activities

Sword Fight

Write the theme for this lesson on a slip of paper. Place that slip of paper, along with the slips of paper from the previous lessons' sword fights, in a bag or hat. One person "draws his sword" (figuratively) and quotes the verse that goes with that theme. then they switch roles: the second person draws and the first person quotes the corresponding scripture. See the introduction under "Its Focus" for a complete explanation.

Palm Branches

Out of large pieces of green construction paper, cut palm branches. Fringe the edges. You may write the memory verse on them if you wish. Then act out the story or sing praise songs and wave the palm branches. Discuss Reading 1.

Communion

Mix grape juice from concentrate and bake flat bread. Mix 1 c. flour, 1/3 c. shortening, ½ tsp. salt and 2 Tbs. water. Bake at 400 degrees for 10-12 minutes. Talk about what these mean. Share communion together, thanking Jesus for giving his life for us and for rising again. Discuss Reading 2.

Windowbox Garden

Plant flower seeds in paper cups and set them in the window. Water them and watch them grow. Talk about the life that is in the seed, even when the seed looks dead. Then discuss Reading 3 (Garden of Gethsemane) and Reading 5 (resurrection).

Sponge Painted Cross

Use black paint, colored construction paper and sponges cut into 4"x1" sections. Draw a hill on the paper. Put the paint onto a plate or bowl so that it just covers the bottom. Press the sponge into the paint and then press it onto the paper, first vertically, then horizontally so that it makes a cross. Paint three crosses on the hill, if you wish. Discuss Reading 4.

Clay-scape of the Garden

Make a clay or play dough landscape of the garden where the tomb was. Leave the "stone" door rolled away from the tomb, and leave the tomb empty. If you wish, children may tell the story to someone else using small toy figures or clothespin figures. Discuss Reading 5.

LESSON 31

Theme: Honesty

Verse: "Do not lie to each other." Colossians. 3:9
(Write this verse on paper swords, one for each
child. Older children can write it themselves.)

Reading 1:   II Kings 5:9-27—Gehazi Lies to Naaman

Questions:

- Why is it important to tell the truth?
- Can you trust someone who lies?
- Who lied in the reading?
- What happened?
- Is it always easy to tell the truth?
- Tell about a time when you or someone else
  told the truth even though it was hard.

Reading 2:   Genesis 12:10-20—Abraham Lies about Sarah

Reading 3:   Genesis 27:1-41—Jacob Deceives Isaac

Reading 4:   Acts 5:1-11—Ananias and Sapphira

Reading 5:   Exodus 32—Aaron Lies about the Golden Calf

Activities

Sword Fight

Write the theme for this lesson on a slip of paper. Place that slip of paper, along with the slips of paper from the previous lessons' sword fights, in a bag or hat. One person draws a theme and reads it aloud. The other person "draws his sword" (figuratively) and quotes the verse that goes with that theme. Then they switch roles: the second person draws and the first person quotes the corresponding scripture. See the introduction under "Its Focus" for a complete explanation.

Lies in Ads

Look at the advertisements in newspapers and magazines. Ask if each statement in the ad is true or not. Look for lies. Discuss the lies we hear in tv and radio ads. Why do advertisers tell us that theirs is the best product, or that we deserve this, or that we can't live without that, or that this will make us happy or good looking or lovable?

Deception

Do a magic trick for the children. To prepare for the trick, pour a pint of hot water into a jar. Add ½ cup of salt and stir to dissolve. Pour a pint of room temperature water into another jar. To perform the trick, put an egg into the water that is room temperature. Now take the egg out and wave your hand over it. Put it into the salty water. What happens? Is this magic? Let the children try it. Discuss lies. Is there a difference between tricks and lies? Is there a difference between teasing and lying?

Idols Today

Look in magazines and catalogues to find pictures of things we could consider idols today. (Things we spend our time pursuing; that we put our trust in; that we are tempted to value more than a relationship with God.) Cut them out and glue them to a large piece of construction paper. Discuss Reading 5 and lies.

Guess the Lie

On a piece of paper, each person writes three facts about himself. (His likes and dislikes, or his talents, or shoe or shirt size, etc.) He must make up one of these facts, so that one "fact" among the three is a lie. Now each person tells, one at a time, the three "facts" about himself. The others try to guess which "fact" is a lie. Discuss lies.

Rebus

On a piece of paper, the child writes Proverbs 23:15-16, except that when he comes to a word that can be drawn instead of written, he draws a picture of it. For example, he draws a heart instead of writing "heart." He can write "w+" and then draw eyes to make the word "wise." And so on. Discuss lying.

LESSON 32

Theme: Forgiving

Verse: "Forgive as the Lord forgave you." Col. 3:13
(Write this verse on paper swords, one for each
child. Older children can write it themselves.)

Reading 1:   Luke 15:11-24—The Prodigal Son

Questions:

- Why do we need to forgive people?
- Is it always easy to forgive someone?
- How do we show we forgive?
- Who forgave in the reading?
- Tell of a time when you forgave someone or someone forgave you.

Reading 2:   Genesis 27:41 and chapters 32 and 33—Esau Forgives

Reading 3:   Luke 7:36-50—Woman Anoints Jesus

Reading 4:   Matthew 18:21-35—70 x 7 and the Unforgiving Servant

Reading 5:   Luke 23:32-34—Jesus on the Cross Forgives

Activities

Sword Fight

Write the theme for this lesson on a slip of paper. Place that slip of paper, along with the slips of paper from the previous lessons' sword fights, in a bag or hat. One person draws a theme and reads it aloud. The other person "draws his sword" (figuratively) and quotes the verse that goes with that theme. Then they switch roles: the second person draws and the first person quotes the corresponding scripture. See the introduction under "Its Focus" for a complete explanation.

Prodigal Son Party

Bake and decorate cupcakes. Decorate the room or yard with balloons and streamers. Discuss Reading 1 and have a party to celebrate forgiveness.

Verse Puzzle

Write the memory verse on a piece of construction paper. Cut it like a jigsaw puzzle, but in large pieces. Let the children try to put it together again. Or each child can make his own puzzle and then trade with someone else to try to work that person's puzzle. Discuss forgiveness.

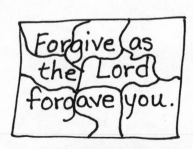

Act it Out

Act out the story of the Prodigal Son or the Unforgiving Servant. Towels, old pillowcases and scarves can be costumes. Discuss forgiveness.

Jacob's Travel Mural

On a long piece of butcher paper or adding machine tape, the children draw the caravan that Jacob took with him when he went back to his home and met Esau. Reading 2 will tell you what order the family walked in when they went to meet Esau. Discuss forgiveness.

Crosses

Glue popsicle sticks together to make a cross. (Popsicle sticks may be called craft sticks at craft stores and school supply stores.) Write on the cross "FORGIVE."

LESSON 33

Theme: Courage II

Verse: "Be strong and courageous." II Chronicles
                 32:7a
                 (Write this verse on paper swords, one for each
                 child. Older children can write it themselves.)

Reading 1:   Exodus 2:1-10—Miriam and the Princess

Questions:
                 • Is fear the opposite of courage, or can you be
                   courageous and afraid at the same time?
                 • Who was brave in the reading?
                 • Who gives us strength and courage?
                 • Tell about a time when you or someone else
                   showed courage.

Reading 2:   Exodus 14:5-31—Crossing the Red Sea

Reading 3:   Joshua 6:1-20—Marching around Jericho

Reading 4:   II Chronicles 20:1-25—Jehoshaphat

Reading 5:   II Kings 7:3-16—Lepers at the Aramean Camp
                 (read chapter 6 as background)

Activities

Sword Fight

Write the theme for this lesson on a slip of paper. Place that slip of paper, along with the slips of paper from the previous lessons' sword fights, in a bag or hat. One person draws a theme and reads it aloud. The other person "draws his sword" (figuratively) and quotes the verse that goes with that theme. Then they switch roles: the second person draws and the first person quotes the corresponding scripture. See the introduction under "Its Focus" for a complete explanation.

Soap Flake Sea

With a hand mixer, mix Ivory Soap flakes clothes detergent with water added a little at a time. Mix in blue food coloring. Spoon it out on paper plates and let the children fingerpaint it into "waves" to look like a sea. Everyone must be careful not to rub their eyes. Let these dry, or tell the story with toy figures or clothespin figures, making a path through the "waves" at the appropriate time. Discuss Reading 2.

Siphoning Water

Use two containers and a long, flexible plastic tube. Fill one container with water and put one end of the tube into it. Gently suck on the other end of the tube to start the water flowing through it and then quickly put the tube into the second container. Experiment with it. What configuration of containers and tube works best? How did God move the water at the Red Sea? Discuss Reading 2.

Water Surface

Fill a glass with water right up to the rim. Now let children gently drop coins into the glass one at a time. Watch the surface of the water round up. How many coins will go into the full glass before the water spills over the sides? The water has a surface "tension" where the molecules bond together. That's how it can stay in the glass for awhile, even though it rounds up higher than the glass. Discuss Reading 2 and courage.

Battle Song

Give the children this assignment. You are in the choir of Jehoshaphat's army. You are going to march out to battle. Write a battle song to sing while you march. Discuss Reading 4 and courage.

Domino Tumble

Set dominoes on their short ends, one behind the other, making any pattern you wish. Try to use all the dominoes. Then tap the one at the very end and watch them all tumble quickly, one by one. Discuss Reading 3 and courage.

LESSON 34

Theme: Finding Out (Curiosity, Looking for Answers)

Verse: "Seek and you will find." Matthew 7:7
(Write this verse on paper swords, one for each
child. Older children can write it themselves.)

Reading 1:   II Chronicles 9:1-12—The Queen of Sheba

Questions:

- Why do people ask questions?
- What kind of person asks questions?
- Is it all right to ask questions?
- Who was wanting to find out something in the reading?
- How did they find out what they wanted to know?
- Are there things that would be dangerous to find out about?
- Tell about something you'd like to find out.
- Tell about a question you'd like to ask God.

Reading 2:   I Kings 4:29-34—Solomon's Learning

Reading 3:   John 3:1-21—Nicodemus

Reading 4:   II Kings 22:1-23:3—Josiah and the Law

Reading 5:   Nehemiah 2:1-18—Nehemiah Inspects the Walls

Activities

Sword Fight

Write the theme for this lesson on a slip of paper. Place that slip of paper, along with the slips of paper from the previous lessons' sword fights, in a bag or hat. One person draws a theme and reads it aloud. The other person "draws his sword" (figuratively) and quotes the verse that goes with that theme. Then they switch roles: the second person draws and the first person quotes the corresponding scripture. See the introduction under "Its Focus" for a complete explanation.

A New Animal

Pretend you are an explorer and just discovered a new animal. Draw the animal you discovered and give it a name. Discuss Reading 2 and curiosity.

Story by Candlelight

Do reading 3 at night with the lights off and only a candle to light the room. Discuss the reading.

Flashlight Stars

Tape a piece of cardboard or a black piece of construction paper over the end of a flashlight. With a pin, punch holes in the paper so that the light will shine through. If you wish, find pictures of some constellations and punch the holes to look like a constellation. In the dark, shine the stars onto a wall. Discuss Reading 3.

Scroll Rolls

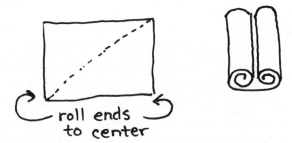

roll ends to center

Use refrigerated crescent roll dough. Leave two of the triangles together to form a rectangle. Roll this rectangle up from both ends at once so the rolls from each end meet in the middle. This makes a scroll. Bake according to package directions. Discuss Reading 4.

Play Dough Brick Walls

Make small bricks out of play dough or clay. Stack them up to make city walls. Discuss Reading 5.

LESSON 35

Theme: Helping (Serving)

Verse: "Serve (help) one another in love."
                   Galalatians 5:13
                   (Write this verse on paper swords, one for each
                   child. Older children can write it themselves.)

Reading 1:   Genesis 2:18-22—Eve, Adam's Helper

Questions:
                   • What kinds of jobs do we think of when we
                     think of people who serve others?
                   • Will serving others help us get to heaven?
                   • Why do we serve people?
                   • Can we serve others even if we don't have a
                     job?
                   • Name some ways we can serve or help.
                   • Tell of a time when you served (helped)
                     someone or someone served you.
                   • Who served or helped in the reading, and
                     how?

Reading 2:   Exodus 17:8-16—Moses' Hands Raised

Reading 3:   Exodus 18:1-27—Helpers for Moses

Reading 4:   Luke 6:12-16—Jesus Chooses Apostles

Reading 5:   Acts 9:19-25—Paul let down in a Basket

Activities

Sword Fight

Write the theme for this lesson on a slip of paper. Place that slip of paper, along with the slips of paper from the previous lessons' sword fights, in a bag or hat. One person draws a theme and reads it aloud. The other person "draws his sword" (figuratively) and quotes the verse that goes with that theme. Then they switch roles: the second person draws and the first person quotes the corresponding scripture. See introduction under "Its Focus" for a complete explanation.

Coupon Book

Fold typing paper into thirds and then into half. Unfold and cut along the folds. Stack these pieces of paper together and staple or punch two holes in the ends and tie yarn through the holes. On each of these pages, the child writes or draws something he will do to help his parents. He gives the coupon book to them, and when they present him with a coupon, he does whatever he has written on it. Discuss serving.

Paper Cup Phones

Discuss the different ways you help each other as you make this phone. Punch a small hole in the center of the bottoms of the cups. Cut a 20-30 foot piece of kite string. Run one end of the string through the hole in one cup. Run the other end of the string through the hole in the other cup. Tie the ends of string to used match sticks. One person holds one cup to his ear.

Another person holds the other cup to his mouth. They walk apart, stretching the string tightly. One person talks and the other listens. Discus people who serve by calling and encouraging others. Discuss Reading 3.

Hand Traced Tree

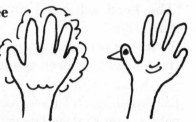

Trace around hands on construction paper. The children use crayons or markers to make trees or clowns or animals out of their hand prints. Discuss Reading 2.

Basket Rubbing

Have a variety of baskets available. Children place typing paper over a basket and rub a crayon over the paper to make the design of the basket show through. They can use one piece of paper for each basket or rub over small sections of each basket on one piece of paper. Discuss Reading 5.

Woven Wreath

Discuss how you help (serve) each other during this project. Cut 36"x1" strips of fabric. Tie three of them together at the top. The children braid these and tie them again at the bottom. Make this braid into a circle and sew or staple the ends together to form a wreath. Weave ribbon in and out of the wreath if you want. Discuss how people weave baskets and discuss Reading 5.

LESSON 36

Theme: God's Plan and Purpose for Our Lives

Verse: "The Lord will fulfill his purpose for me."
Psalm 138:8
(Write this verse on paper swords, one for each
child. Older children can write it themselves.)

Reading 1:   Exodus 2:10, 3:7-10—Moses, trained in the
palace, sent to negotiate with Pharaoh, and to
lead God's people

Questions:

- What purpose and plan did God have for the
person in the reading?
- How did God prepare him for that purpose?
- Does God still have purposes and plans for
people?
- Does God prepare people?
- What do you think a part of God's plan or
purpose for your life might be?

Reading 2:   I Samuel 2:18-21—Samuel, trained in the
temple, grew up to be a prophet

Reading 3:   I Samuel 17:34-37—David, trained to lead and
defend sheep, grew to be king and warrior

Reading 4:   Daniel 1:3-4, 17; 2:48-49—Daniel, trained with
nobility in Israel, called to be a wise man in
Babylon

Reading 5:   Acts 22:2-3, 22-29; 9:1-19—Paul (Saul), trained
in the scriptures, both Jewish and Roman citi-
zen, called to be a missionary

Activities

Sword Fight

Write the theme for this lesson on a slip of
paper. Place that slip of paper, along with the
slips of paper from the previous lessons' sword
fights, in a bag or hat. One person draws a
theme and reads it aloud. The other person
"draws his sword" (figuratively) and quotes the
verse that goes with that theme. Then they
switch roles: the second person draws and the
first person quotes the corresponding scripture.
See the introduction under "Its Focus" for a
complete explanation.

Silhouettes

Stand the child sideways in front of a strong light
source (like a slide camera or lamp) so that the
silhouette of his face is projected onto the wall.
Tape a black piece of paper up where the
silhouette is and draw around the silhouette.
Cut it out and let the child glue it to another color
of paper and write his name under it, along with
the memory verse.

Profile

The child places his head sideways against a
large piece of manila paper. Trace around his
profile. He then draws things that are special to
him inside the "head." For example, his favorite
food, favorite color, sport, animal, etc. Discuss

God's work in the lives of the people in the readings and God's work in the child's life.

Cup Puppets

Choose a person from one of the readings to make into a puppet. Use styrofoam cups. Turn them upside down and glue yarn on for hair. Glue on buttons for eyes or use markers to draw features. Glue on beard, if you want. Headbands, veils or scarves can be made of fabric. To operate the puppet, the child sticks his hand into the cup. Discuss the God's work in the lives of the people that you chose to make into puppets.

Raisin Face Biscuit

Use canned refrigerated biscuit dough, or make biscuit dough. Let the child place raisins on top to make a face. Bake according to package directions. Discuss people from the readings and how God works in people's lives and has a plan for everyone.

Fruit Face

Slice various kinds of fruits. On a plate, the child arranges the fruit so that it makes a face. For example, banana slices could be eyes, apple could be mouth, orange sections for ears, strawberry for nose, etc. The child can use his imagination. Discuss how God works in people's lives and has a plan for everyone.

OTHER ALLEN THOMAS PUBLICATIONS
by
Karyn Henley

Snip-Its   Bible Stories told with Scissors and Paper

First Hand   Cooking, Science and Dramatic Play

First Hand   Arts and Crafts

First Hand   Creative Storytelling

Great God, Grateful Child   A Curriculum for Bible Class

OTHER PUBLISHERS

The Beginner's Bible (Questar Publishers, Inc.)

Hatch! (Carolrhoda Books)

Call or write for a free catalog or for information regarding Karyn's teacher training workshops:

Allen Thomas Publishing
Post Office Box 40269
Nashville, TN 37204

(615) 385-9073